There Is Something About Being An Episcopalian

SAINT JULIAN PRESS

POETRY

PRAISE for…THERE IS SOMETHING ABOUT BEING AN EPISCOPALIAN

"Ron Starbuck is poet who has taken to heart and soul the teaching in Psalm 46, 'Be still and know that I am God.' Spoken in the voice of a deep listener, who seeks to embrace all souls in the Mystery of God's Love, who seeks to heal the breach. These poems are ecumenical both in that they are unifying and in the etymological root of the word, which is derived from the Greek word for house. Here is poetry that beautifully and prayerfully makes of the world a home where all of us may dwell."

~ Aliki Barnstone, University of Missouri

"Ron Starbuck has written a work of extraordinary vision and prophecy; this is a book of both profound reverence and a song of contemporary liturgy. It is a masterpiece that will transform the belief and devotion of all who experience these lines, either verbally or literally. Without doubt, this is a great work for the new Twenty-First Century."

~ Kevin McGrath, Harvard University

OTHER BOOKS

BY

RON STARBUCK

WHEN ANGELS ARE BORN
WHEELS TURNING INWARD

THERE IS SOMETHING ABOUT BEING AN EPISCOPALIAN

NEW & SELECTED POEMS

BY

RON STARBUCK

SAINT JULIAN PRESS

HOUSTON

Published by
SAINT JULIAN PRESS, Inc.
2053 Cortlandt, Suite 200
Houston, Texas 77008

www.saintjulianpress.com

ISBN-13: 978-0-9965231-7-2
ISBN-10: 0-9965231-7-0
Library of Congress Control Number: 2016906673

Cover Art & Design
by Ron Starbuck
Stained Glass Image
Trinity Episcopal Church Midtown Houston

Author's Photo Credit: Mary Beth Touchstone

Some Day, In The Emergence From This Fierce Insight,
Let Me Sing Jubilation And Praise To Assenting Angels.

DUINO ELEGIES ~ THE TENTH ELEGY

RAINER MARIA RILKE

CONTENTS

FORWARD

RON STARBUCK writes in the Christian tradition of vision and enlightenment and in this prophetic book the poetry of *being* that is *Episcopalian* is expressed from the point of view of a *théoros*, that is, from the perspective of one who witnesses and contemplates the truth of the cosmos: all that is immaterial, indestructible, and permanently unchanging. It is upon this view that the present book has been created.

This is a remarkable work for a Twenty-First Century where secular and pragmatic thinking so dominates Western culture; for the words and sentiments of this book are strongly within the vein of an early English spiritual tradition: *The Cloud Of Unknowing* or *The Fire Of Love*, for instance. There, the union of lover and beloved assumes more than metaphorical standing and becomes indicative of that which cannot actually be expressed *via* human speech. This is the ultimate paradox of the work, a dilemma which Dante himself faced at the centre of the cosmic Rose in the *Paradiso*: how to speak of that single point of time which is endless and unfinished and always beyond the domain of human language.

There is a terrific humility or *kénosis* in these poems for this is an extended song not only of belief but also of knowledge and within these lines are expressed an experience that is both earthly and supernal, one that is both human and otherworldly. The faithful modesty that is portrayed here is one of admiration at the reception and presence of its universal viewing, of angels, stars, suns, and human vicissitude; yet the voice which composes these lines is one fully situated in an emotion of compassion.

Much of the poetry is *oecumenical* in outlook in that the poet is obviously deeply informed by the early Greek tradition of the Eastern or Orthodox Church; and likewise, the poet is comfortable in certain basic foundational concepts of early Buddhism. Starbuck is a learned individual and carries his wisdom easily yet this book is by no means an exclusive or dogmatic showing for it is firstly the fruit of unworldly occurrence rather than of any formal teaching.

It is from the experience of prayer and of ritual communion that Starbuck has drawn his images and sentiments. His position as devotee is not one that is wholly directed toward the Christ but goes further: the author expresses his silent aspiration as would the Christ himself as he prayed at Gethsemane. That is, the prayer is directed at the First Person of the Trinity, the Father, not primarily at the Christ figure, and in this the language actually becomes aniconic. It is this which makes the book extraordinary and its transcendent distinction so unique.

In fact, if this book were to be performed by solo voice the effect would be one that was liturgical in form, such is the enactment and transition which the poetry effects. This is a literature of belief and devotion, of vision and of mystical engagement, and the work possesses both the *tempo* and fusion which expresses such a paradigm of divine office. The words sustain a transparency and clarity which allows the reader—or an audience—to pass through the language and move towards what is being made visible for the soul's apprehension; and as such, this is the perception and effort of great and terrific mastery.

All this is of course ultimately founded upon the psychic presence of the human heart, the fact that human affection—its vagaries and ordeals—for us is the first station of all desire in the cosmos: human love is thus the initial condition of vital and living metaphor. This is the final refinement of the book of Starbuck and as such it is not an object for aesthetic appreciation but a lens for active reverence.

Kevin McGRATH, Harvard University, Two Thousand *&* Sixteen

❖

The light of the body is the eye. If therefore thine eye be single, thy whole body shall be full of light.

MATTHEW 6:22

21st Century King James Version

There Is Something About Being An Episcopalian

I. SEEING THROUGH THE EYE'S OF CHRIST

THERE IS SOMETHING ABOUT BEING AN EPISCOPALIAN

There is something
about
being an Episcopalian.
Something that draws me,
engages me,
moves me forward,
makes me think,
and makes me quake.
There is something there,
something that defines me,
embraces me,
holds me wholly
and holy still,
within, thy stillness.

Something, that rings true
across and through the mind.
Something that touches,
that binds and almost breaks,
that bends a heart,
to hear a voice.
Something that knows a love,
and feels a joy,
that sees a mystery
to which I smile,
as you smile back.

God in heaven
we are a community
that one day soon.

I hope;
I pray,
will know no bounds
or boundaries
in this world.
Thy kingdom
comes;
thy will,
will be done,
on earth
as much
as in heaven.

Unexpectedly
it may seem to some
in spite
of all we fear to do
or do not do.
By your good grace,
thy kingdom comes,
ready or not,
here it comes,
within us,
all around us.
It comes with
or without expectation,
time to wake up.

Now!

GOD'S LONGING

It isn't known when it began,
God's longing,
certainly no one mortal knows.
The angels might know,
but for most, it is still a heavenly secret,
a mystery of mysteries
long hidden.

Some would say that it was always there,
has always been there,
from the first instant,
long before the big bang.
Banged!

Leading up to the first
thought that caused
creation, to explode suddenly
out of the emptiness and nothingness
of all reality, which is still expanding,
still growing
still arising within us each.

Many would say, and I would be one,
that God's longing is eternal.
It is a deep longing, a true longing,
a longing that lingers slowly
and perfectly
stretching out far past our own imaginations.
However, far back or forward we are able to imagine.

It is almost as if God suddenly awoke
and being alone.
In knowing loneliness from the beginning
sighed deeply, sighed so deeply
in that loneliness,
that in breathing out
some portion of God's breath left
his body and being
to seed all creation.

Perhaps it was then, in that moment
when the breath of God first moved
across the waters of earth
or moved through the depths of
nothingness giving birth to creation.
Or gave breath to both Adam and Eve,
and then to all humanity.

Sometimes a thought crosses my mind,
a single thought, born out of my own breath,
as I breathe in deeply during meditation
and out once again quietly and stilly.

Sometimes it comes to me then, in a split second
that this was when God's Holy Spirit first appeared
and continues to appear throughout all history.
I even imagine that in some secret way
my own loneliness and longing are helping to give birth
to God's Holy Spirit

and the compassionate loving-kindness
that follows God's gift to all humankind.
I know this much, that God's longing for us
runs so deep
and so true
that He gave up His only begotten Son, even unto death.
So that we might come to know Him and He us,
and that by this miracle of love
God's Holy Spirit comes to dwell and rest in us.

PRAYERS

I will tell you where prayers come
from, if you will listen.
They travel from one human heart
to another.
They arise unspoken from
the spirit.

They move across the immeasurable
thought filled possibilities
of all things within creation.

Slipping silently between
the stars in quantum reflections.

Every thought is a prayer, thus
we pray unceasingly. Unknowingly
they take flight, pause in belief.
And are gathered together by angels
and archangels of light.
Passing through constellations
known and unknown,
seen and unseen, visible and invisible.

Who then carry them inward into
the veiled memory of the divine
who dwells within.
Who has always dwelled within,
discerned in prayer.

KÝRIE ELÉISON

Lord, have mercy.
Christ, have mercy.

Kýrie Eléison ~ Christe Eléison

I have seen thy holy
places in the Old City
of Jerusalem.
I have walked the
cobblestones Christ
once walked.

I have stood before
each station of the cross
and marked the time
of day you stood there
in pain and agony.

I have felt the hurt of all
thy people, be they
Christian, Jew, or Muslim
from any sect across
the Holy Land.

Kýrie Eléison ~ Christe Eléison

I have been to the Western
Wall and heard it wailing,
crying out in prayer for some
compassion,
some small mercy.

As I have seen your
people praying in the mosques
upon the Temple Mount ~
Al Haram esh-Sahrif, the
Noble Sanctuary.

Each is claimed by many
as a holy site.
So many, O Lord.

I think that there is
nothing here, we may
claim completely as our own,
that is ours.
There is nothing
here that any may claim
that is not yours first.

I hear them crying
on all sides for these
their holy places,
but not yours,
O Lord.

Kýrie Eléison ~ Christe Eléison

I have seen them
bend their
words and
intentions, their
prayers, into
something far
from holy.

I have seen
and heard
them miss the mark
more than once,
in their quest for
your holiness, your
presence in
their life.

Lord God, I wonder
when will we ever
learn that
true holiness is not
found
within these
places alone,
these monuments
and
images of you,
who are
unseen and invisible,
without image.

Kýrie Eléison ~ Christe Eléison

Lord, I wonder when
they will find your
holiness
resting in themselves
as an
indwelling of
the Spirit,
the Holy Spirit.

There was an
infant child
once born upon
a holy night,
a silent night.

Who rested in a
humble manger,
where cattle fed, where
ox and ass and sheep
all dwelled.
The innocent
of creation. Where angels,
shepherds and wise men
bowed in homage to a
new born king, a heavenly
kingdom only, not of this
earth or world.

Kýrie Eléison ~ Christe Eléison

Let us give birth too,
in this most holy of nights,
in the silence and stillness
of this night to the
Christ child
that dwells within
us all.

Kýrie Eléison ~ Christe Eléison

of a memory
that has
faded

in reflection
in knowing
where we

only desire
to be
known

RUMI

Beginning in the first moments
after the Sufi poet Rumi was born
pieces of him over time, began
dissolving into all the elements of earth

like sugar in water, and to this very day
he is with us still, we breathe his breath
in the air, we taste his words
in food grown from our good earth

we find the essence of his verses
floating like seeds of light
locked inside the molecules from his
body and being in the very water we drink

his verses when spoken out loud
are an invocation to the Holy Spirit
they ripen us like wheat
for a harvest of the heart

his words are written inside the chambers of our
hearts like a holy sacrament, he who searched for
God the beloved, or Allah if you wish, in church
and shrine and mosque, to find him finally

tucked inside the pocket of his own heart
can we as Christian, Jew, or Muslim
do any less, to bring an everlasting
peace unto the world, to be as one.

EPHPHATHA

our selves are legion
gathered together in
a single life

and something more
of colors
bright from a billion

stars and nights
we are all blooming
with light

in and through and with
one another
within a single cactus blossom

time and self shaping
both past and future
from a moment found now

the past is never set
nor the future completely
known or fated

both are fluid and
may change
in an openness

a clown's compassion for any child
will transform the past
create eternity here and now

and send it out across
all possibilities and future times
transformation crosses time

and a single smile shared
between a clown and
child will transform it all

the self you knew becomes a new self known
intimately sought - our selves our legion
ephphatha - be opened

ON THE THIRD MORNING
John 20:1-18 and Luke 24:1-12

On the third morning
The women came first,
Somehow knowing in their wisdom
As women often do!
Anxious with sorrow,
Walking in the stillness of night
Just before dawn
And the movement of day.

They came,
Looking for their Lord.
Where they found the stone turned,
Rolled from His tomb.
Their Lord's body gone,
Taken away!

Two disciples came later, to learn
That this was more than an "idle tale,"
Of women, unbelieved.
When entering the tomb, they too saw

The linens that once wrapped His body,
Lying where he was laid. Then
Returned home in amazement,
Not recalling the scriptures
Or the words of Jesus,
Even the one whom he most loved.

While Mary stayed, weeping outside, to
See angels sitting in the tomb
Where once her Lord's body lay.
Jesus speaks, calling Mary by name after asking;
"Woman, why do you weep?
Whom do you seek?

The living are not
Among the dead."
She sees him now, Rabbouni, her teacher,
Moving to embrace him, at last knowing his face
and voice.
He says; "Hold me not, for I must ascend to my Father.
Go, and tell my brothers, what you have seen and heard."

He has Risen, He has Risen!
He has risen from the places of the dead and dying,
He has risen from the solitude of the tomb.
He has Risen, to his Father and our Father.
He has Risen, to his God and our God.
Hallelujah, Christ is Risen!

Let us rise as well, above the noises and distractions of life
to understand that God calls us too to death and
resurrection.
Calling us to die immeasurable times;
To die daily in ourselves.

Let there be a death to our egos and selfishness,
A death to our poverty of spirit and faithlessness,
A death to doubt, hopelessness, and sorrow,
A death to grief where grief can no longer be borne,
A death to intolerance and "the wish to kill,"
A death to violence and war, and fearful hearts,
A death to abused and unloved hearts.

Let there be a death to it all.
Let the illusion and suffering of life be washed away
by the Passion of Christ, creating in us the mind of Christ!

So that we me may join with Him
In many Resurrections,
Let there be Resurrections upon Resurrections
One after another and another,
let there be resurrections without end.

CHRISTMAS CRÈCHE

It comes each winter
after the long darkness,
the light returns.

I have travelled now
to a town older
than memory,

to an undiscovered
countryside claimed by several
languages and faiths.

I have slept in the
crèche of Christ amongst
the dung and dust,

humbled by animals
mute in speech, not
in spirit.

Witnessed by
wise men, shepherds
and angelic hosts,

laid in a manger,
a crib for something
new and needed.

I have cried softly for
their children ~ Christian, Jew,
Muslim;

some who barely understand
the revelation of God's enigma
left uncovered and veiled.

If I could tell you the truth
of Christmas, believe me
I would.

Listen, hear it in
the silence and stillness
of the self.

We've lost so much,
all the mystery and truth,
the deepest meaning

wrung out of the
story in a tirade
of religious literalism.

There are sacred stories
and places in the world,
meant to be internalized

and in doing so a
deeper certainty nearly
always laid bare.

Like the Christ child
left swaddled and
unadorned, resting,

hidden just outside
the City of David, Bethlehem.
God's love being

born into the world
once more, each
Christmas morn.

THE JESUS PRAYER FLAG

this morning, quite early
in fact,
an hour or so after dawn
while walking to my office

i saw a parking garage attendant
in the courthouse district
of downtown Houston
waiving a red-orange
traffic flag
back and forth
back and forth
with the word
JESUS
written there

there he was
waving Jesus around
for all the world to see
he was waving Jesus
like a
Tibetan Buddhist prayer flag
flying in the wind
stirring up the Holy Spirit

he was waving Jesus as a message
as a hope
as a charity
as a blessing
as a reminder
in remembrance
so that we might

wake up and
remember too

if you listened
carefully
clearly
you can hear
the voices
of the homeless
the poor
the imprisoned on parole
the weary
like voices from heaven
as they too passed
by

saying ...

Come, Lord Jesus
Come, Lord Jesus
Come, Lord Jesus

uttering his name without pause
as a prayer, as a song, as a thought

in the back of my mind I can hear them singing

"Jesus loves me this I know
so the Bible tells me so."
I'm sure it was a prayer
a cry from heaven even,
it must have been

for I heard the voices too,
the voices of angels
appearing and arising
as unexpected messengers
as strangers,

and

I think I saw Jesus smiling,
I'm sure I did,
in the smiles on their faces

as I passed by looking, seeing
but staying quiet all the same
not a whisper crossing my lips
not even a small hello.

But certainly a smile, and a hint of some
blessing unasked for,
grace given freely
freely accepted.

A witness to
God's compassion
at work
in the world,
the Kingdom
of God
coming closer
and closer
each day.

THEOSIS

It is hard work
this praxis of union with God.
Who knows how long it will take,

some say a lifetime.
Buddhists and Hindus say several,
theirs may be the longer road it seems.

I am afraid that
I have no patience, of flesh and bone
to wait that long, God calls unceasingly.

I know this,
that each time I partake
in Holy Communion, Christ comes.

Each time I hear the Eucharistic words
of thanksgiving spoken,
each time I feel the mystery of
the Holy Spirit descending.

Each time I open
my hands and heart
in stillness and sacrament,
Christ comes

With a soft and gentle
intensity beyond all words
to tell.

It is not a simple thing to tell at all.
God it seems, is always waiting in the wings,
such divine grace is always given
as a gift unearned.

Whenever I open my hands, even now
in this very instant,
as during Eucharist,
Christ comes
in this moment of epiclesis.

To land lightly, like a dove, in each palm
held upward in reverence, in prayer,
becoming a reflection of holiness
that travels throughout my whole being
binding his spirit to my flesh and bone.

Opening my whole self,
filling my own broken body with a light, that blooms
to transform all truth, reality itself.

Tongues of flame
burning brightly with a radiance,
as on the day of Pentecost.

To become one with Christ,
as Eve was once joined to Adam
"bone of his bone and flesh of his flesh."

II. Seeing Through The Eyes Of Buddha & Jesus

A MOCKINGBIRD'S SONG

There are moments,
like this morning,
when my heart is so full
it has become the song of the

Mockingbird singing outside our windows.
Who may sing at any time day or night, its song
of wonder and making.
Who is binding the world together

with each single and heart-making note, whose
songs are as bright as God's love for all of creation.
It is 4:42 AM precisely now,
at such and such longitude and latitude.

And I am sitting in a chair
typing as quickly as I can these
words arising out of the emptiness or nothingness
of my own being, alive with wonder.

So that no single word may escape the
motion of my mind, which in
this moment is like a razor's edge,
sharp and clearly defined.

The mockingbird is still singing its song, which you may
easily imagine moving up through its gentle heart, and
throat, and out through its voice, to spin again and again
up and around this fragile world, our home.

The song of its being is still winding its way
into the many mansions of my heart,
opening my heart to the mystery of its
word and voice.

On Friday our neighbor delivered to Joanne,
a bouquet of lilies, Easter Lilies in May.
Oh, more than a dozen I imagine now.
And then yesterday Joanne bought home

even more flowers.
Carnations and mums for church today,
so the house is full of their fragrance,
along with the smell of my morning coffee.

If the self is constantly changing,
from one moment to the next
as my Buddhist friends tell me.
If the self is so impermanent as

to be not-self, or no-self, anattā *(uhn-uht-tah)*.
Why is it then that I feel so
completely and utterly
alive in this very moment?

Why is it that I can still
hear the song of the mockingbird
entering my heart?
Raising it up again and again

like a sacrament,
to the wonders of creation,
to this gift we call life.
Why is it that this one song never

seems to leave me from
one hallowed moment to the next?
Why is the song more, much more,
than a vague and distant memory?

Maybe as the Buddha suggests, this is
a question we should put aside for now, not to worry.
And just to be as we are, to answer or say neither
yes or no, to live in the mystery perhaps.

Still, wherever you may be this morning, whatever you
may be doing, stop now. Stop and take one deep breath,
breathing in slowing and fully, and out once again.
Stop, and realize if nothing else, that you are alive.

And that within your own heart is the same song, of the
same mockingbird, in the very same tree outside our
window that is singing through our own hearts, binding us
together as one human family, a family of humanity.

Let this one moment become a beginning, a healing,
a grace, a passage from one human heart to the next.
Where the world is made new and whole, where we know
with a certainty marked by compassion.

Where we come to see Christ, and even the
Buddha, alive in one another.

COMPOSING THE FIRST GRACE

Early this morning
I was sitting
on our front porch,

coffee in hand,
when the mockingbirds
suddenly began singing,

composing
the first grace
of the dawn's
light into being,

streaming out
golden threads of light,
their songs
entering

into the
crown opening
of my head,
and from there,

woven all through
my body,
circling down and
then back around

up through each
cell and molecule,
weaving together equally
every note, as sutras'

binding in unity
the bright strands
of my DNA,
and then coming

to rest on a razor's edge
of even more light.
The mind becoming perfectly
formed in its formlessness,

in complete balance, becoming
a bright sphere — ever
expanding,
translucent — clearly

defined, seen
and understood,
unfolding the visible
and invisible mystery

of creation,
knowing and
being
known

"Sometimes at that moment a wave of light breaks into our darkness, and it is as though a voice were saying: "You are accepted. You are accepted, accepted by that which is greater than you, and the name of which you do not know. Do not ask for the name now; perhaps you will find it later. Do not try to do anything now; perhaps later you will do much. Do not seek for anything; do not perform anything; do not intend anything. Simply accept the fact that you are accepted!" —Paul Tillich

TRAVELLERS

I have travelled
From one edge

Of the known
Universe to another

I have slipped silently
Between the stars

Into the secret murmurings
Of nebulas

I have moved from
From one constellation

To another in a
Moment's thought

Sailed through the bright
Centre of a billion suns

And voyaged back again
Just as fast

I have flown with Cygnus the Swan
Hunted with Orion

Touched the invisible
Formlessness of dark energy

And shaped it with God's
Blessing into fresh forms

Seen entire worlds die
And new ones born

Again and
Again

Across all eternity
And everywhere

I was lifted up by
Angels and Archangels who

Followed me
From one

Hallowed place
To another

It's all a miracle
You know, Earth especially

This —still slight point
Held within creation

What miracle will
you discover today?

MOCKINGBIRD MORNING

Early this morning, I listened to the sound
of two mockingbirds singing a duet,
with the composition of their song twisting and

spinning through the air,
like brilliant streams of light.
When I looked up to find them,

I saw the waning moon bright with the
promise of dawn, framed by the branches
of our neighbor's pecan tree,

heavy with new leaves from the spring.
On any morning, we can go out
to one of our two porches

and listen to the clever and soothing songs
of mockingbird, dove, and sparrow.
The robins have returned as well, for now;

they always fly on when the heat of summer comes.
It is early May, and the warm humidity of Southeast
Texas is just beginning to edge up.

Each cool morning now is a gracious gift
we treasure, knowing that the hot days
of summer will soon be coming.

What I want to do most today is to
sit for the longest time listening to the
sounds of the morning, arising out of

the quiet emptiness of the earth. To simply close
my eyes and meditate on each song moving up
through the bones and marrow of my body, and out again

through my breath, binding together each stray atom of
my being into one coherent symphony. This is what God
must feel each moment across one universe to the next,

as endless galaxies and solar systems move timelessly
through the deepness of all creation, spinning out the
one clear song of this, his divine design.

If God, as many believe is love. Then I believe
it must be that our love added to others, is helping
to fashion his one song of creation.

And that if we ever stopped loving, really
stopped loving one another, then the world would
truly end suddenly and sadly with no warning at all.

This is why Christ gave us his two greatest
commandments, and Buddha taught compassion,
because they knew and wanted us to know too.

As long as one single person remembers how
to love and forgive anew each morning, like a child,
then the world is saved again and again.

Each morning becoming a new creation,
as God's Holy Spirit moves across the waters
of our life, and we find our way home to Eden.

IN PERFECT BALANCE

Some day, in the emergence from this fierce insight, let me sing jubilation and
praise to assenting Angels. – Rilke

There is the beauty
of the angels,
and the fear of all our daemons.
But we, we move

between them both;
we dance upon a razor's
edge of perfect light,
in perfect balance.

The mind resting there,
like a brilliant globe
of illumination, the eyes
piercing in their vision,

seeing through all illusion.
They are the same,
angel and daemon.
We are the same.

They are as one, as two lovers
breathing with a single breath,
turning the world
inside out,

in this calling
from the gods,
breathe deep,
breathe deep,

look far, look farther still,
into the eternal
mirrored within
the mind's imagination.

ŚŪNYATĀ
EMPTINESS IS FORM; FORM IS EMPTINESS

Emptiness
is a cupless cup
without shape
formless and lucid
luminous with light.

Precisely positioned
between
heaven and earth,
where the space within
is completely transparent,
unspoken, without words.

Where
a single raindrop
fragile and compliant,
essential in form,
falling quickly or gently
may be caught
and collected,

to be seen
as a reflection
unstated in its purity,
as a thought
arising out of
of our beingness.

Coming into being
faintly glowing at first
as the vividness
of daybreak
becomes brighter,
and brighter.

As we awaken
to each day,
each thought, understood,
explicitly expressed,
guided by wisdom

in the mystery, which is God,
which is creation,
which is infinite,
which is reality,
which we create
from ourselves.

Where we hold
with breathlessness,
many new beginnings,
being and becoming.

Where we hold
each new creation
in the holiness
of the heart.

Arising out of
each sacred moment
of the day,
in the smallest of things,
in kindness freely given
and unasked for,
accepted with graciousness.

In compassion found
in the strangest of places,
almost alien in encounter,
in grace given
out of our desire

to heal and repair
each human heart,
where all people
are one.

Where we empty
ourselves
to become
as one

III. Seeing Through A Poet's Eyes

LE CAMPANE DELLA CHIESA DI VENEZIA
The church bells of Venice

Somewhere the Venetian
moon has hidden itself,
and the saddest songs

of the sea birds
have followed it
far out of sight.

The gulls soaring high, ask
with a questioning cry, when,
when will you ever return?

We answer smiling,
as if to say a part of us
remains, always,

even now — a vision
— a sound, our many
dinner conversations,

embedded, like a sea shell
in the stone steps, where
we walked.

The church bells
of Venice have the longest
memories; we believe.

We linger in time,
endlessly listening to
their sacred sounds,

ringing as they have for
centuries, each bell
in its own solitary voice.

Although, some may say
the sea remembers
even more,

as moon and tide
pull us back
into ourselves.

We hear the bells marking
history with a sound of
laughter and sorrow both,

of yesterdays stretched
along moments uncovered in
intimate interludes.

Each day unfolding fully,
tomorrow patiently waiting
as an actor in the wings,

begging us to remember
each step taken
on the ancient stone

streets, where ten thousand
steps are taken and cross
each other, each day.

Passing by one place
or another, with a sigh,
a troubled lament,

felt, as we stroll hand
in hand over each bridge
and canal.

There is so much to see,
so many memories that
enter into

our sight. We are haunted by
those who have walked here
before.

We are moved by the
remembrance of
ancient beauty,

layered now upon
the bones of our own
memories,

and the sad, sad
songs of the sea birds
calling us back.

VOICES

Voices – Voices

Like the poet, Rilke, with each breath taken, I have heard
and half heard the angels calling out from the depths;

— let them speak, as the whisperings of holy messengers,

in the unfathomable nighttime before dawn, upon the air,
in a quickening of flesh.

These are the forgotten memories we may all one day
recall, more often then we suspect, subtle and obscure,

— traveling on countless pathways of neural light,

crossing our thoughts with distant remembrances that
arise out of the silence of the saints. These are the voices
I heard once before,

— in a church north of Pienza, when we travelled in Italy,

where lighting a candle and bowing her head, Joanne
offered with a sad smile and a small hope, prayers for
a close friend, who was ill at the time,

— struggling in life, and in death, as we all do.

In every church and chapel, we entered that journey,
she repeated the ritual, and in each one, I heard, the
same order of murmuring voices.

Not that I could understand their musings, far from it,
since they spoke only in hushed tones, in the ineffable and
intangible — tongues of angels and heaven.

Verse after verse, follows each breath we breathe; they flow in as a chorus; every word coming quickly, expressed ever so faintly, not always distinct.

Flowing sinuously over the body like soft fallen rain, running over the earth and washing away.

— Vanishing.

And then they return in a shower of lyrics, in a moment, or even years later, each word rushing in with such a haste, anxiously waiting in expectation to take its place.

Out of this silence the poet within conceives unknown – unheard languages of the spirit, new words and verses flowing out unhindered as a blessing.

Encompassing the wonder of life, from the waters of Mnemosyne that pour forth,

— let the memories speak.

Each poet writes in their own angelic tongue, and humankind listens, or they do not. Do you?

Sometimes, the angels speak too fast, and they are rarely kind or generous in their time. We cannot write the words down, quickly — enough.

— Something is always left unwritten.

Words and images, thought after thought, come and go on — it all overflows, and you can never know what the angels may honestly want you to write,

— since they do not speak plainly.

You must seek the beloved; only she can translate
such language as a muse, and something more dwelling
within us.

It is truly unexpected, how even the stars fall
silent in her presence.

One day soon, we will all become fluent
— in her angelic tongue.

BELOVED ONE

Yes, there you are hidden within
these pale amber, rose tint and snowy wings.

Trusting me to discover your eternal beauty, now
visibly known and seen as mystery.

Angel wings enfolded in a pale delicate texture
of softest skin and satin.

Yes, I see you, so clearly now.

Open as you are, waiting in expectation, in this grace
filled moment of adoration and consecration.

Wondering how I lost the memory of your
quiet passionate touch, resting in your subtle divine light,
resting in this timeless moment of reflection.

I am naked again, my long sought soul.
I am immersed, bathed in your light,
your countenance of graciousness.

Bidding me to enter into such a gentle
consciousness of spirit.

As light itself, as honey poured out upon my
humanity, my beloved one - eternal self,
whose light is at no time ever lost.

Here is the self who lives forever captured in
the reminiscence of each constellation affecting
the firmaments, bound together
in heaven's truest realm.

You have broken me open, again and again
with the beauty of being.

By beauty itself, aching to know intimately
the touch of hand and thought.

Casting away all grief I am supple once more,
renewed in the promise of your colours,
your softness and strength.

Knowing you were always there waiting
with patience for me to rediscover this beauty
of the self, ever changing as it is, resting softly like
the reflecting light and color from an angel's wings.

So, we come to know. So, we are ever known.
So, we are born and born again and again
through many lives into this translucent holy light.

THEY HAVE ASKED

They have asked
where is my beloved?

I cannot say where or
when she may appear,

in the darkness or the light,
her memory dwells.

In starlight or sunlight,
she dances a dance; no one knows.

And yet I know her well,
as we have passed together

through and with and
in time eternal.

In music, we are still
together learning,

in rhythmic beats,
known before time was time.

So it is in this still night,
so it is with love unbound.

ENCHANTRESS ~ SOPHIA

Mysterious aspects of the rainbow-colored
spirit in expectations of a future time

in which, all shall be revealed and
truth shown to be

a fantastic vision conjured up by
this enchantress supreme.

She has stolen the wizard's
secret heart and transformed it

into a universe of lost possibilities,
and hidden madness.

And yet, these are, only fantasies of the mind
caught in this single moment of time

Moving together as one,
moving as one person

into a better world.
Where all futures merge into

a oneness with the universe
revealed — unhidden — beyond

all speculations we might imagine.
She comes — she comes,

be aware and rejoice once more.
Sophia, dances across

one universe after another,
they are infinite in our sight,

singularities expanding without
end — reflections of the light.

ALWAYS KNOWN

Dancing on
ribbons
of light,

the fair enchantress
bows with grace
to the old wizard,

to his youth and
vitality poured
into each lotus blossom,

to something new
growing within the world.
To time which is

always ageless,
to the unseen
unremembered,

part of the self
who arises from
subtle memories.

To the enchanted
eyesight
that will cross

forever one universe
after another in
our imaginations.

To carry us all into
undiscovered realms
where the unknown

is revealed, to a kiss
soft and delicate
in its touch,

unfathomed in
its passion,
infinitely celebrated

remembered and
eminently sought;
always known.

OZ

I have been to Kansas
tossed in the air
by strong storms

and landed in Oz
danced with a wizard,
and a good white witch too,

hugged many a Munchkin,
clicked my heels together
three times

and found my
way home, more than once;
many times

And you,
Yes; you,
can you say the same?

Where have all your
travels taken you
in this glad merry world?

WIZARD & WHITEFACE CLOWN
ZEN PRIEST
George Jisho Robertson, a wise old soul and friend, an Anam Cara.

The old wizard
sits with a winsome smile
and a knowing look.

The visage of a wise
whiteface clown
bears its marks

with laugh lines
and wrinkles
well earned.

He has seen so
much of life, known joys
and sorrows,

love always, or nearly
always, deep friendships
and family.

He lights one more
cigarette, not his last
by any means;

a reminiscence perhaps
of an ancient amulet,
a shaman's talisman.

The smoke drifts upwards,
curls around his head
as visions and dreams.

If you look closely, you
may see Buddha sitting
under the Sala tree, or

a Naga Prince sheltered
by a king cobra
in safety from thought

forms without number.
With a piercing vision
he looks up;

his students bow
politely, sit in promise
and smile back.

Nothing is said
between them,
there is no need,

there is only
this moment, here now
complete now.

It happens subtly;
letters and symbols
begin forming

wordlessly; they speak
and then something
breaks through

beyond thought
and form;
silent verses.

Poetic language spoken
between souls, in a single
silent tongue,

in that silence, in
this infinite openness
they rest as one.

One world arises and passes
away, then another
and another,

mirrored in
thought, in breath,
where all

creation moves
in wordless expectation;
in stillness,

to be still and
fully known
as mystery.

THE WIZARD

A wizened wizard traces tranquilly upon
a blank slate — tabula rasa, bows nobly
to his high enchantress whose

wisdom enters into his being, twin
aspects in the self, henceforth divine
compassion reigns.

He caresses his silver beard a time
or two in thoughtfulness and
draws one universe after another.

Each expands, becoming one, then two,
an endless number, unwritten realities
within limitless possibilities.

He pauses, to colour in never-ending stars; galaxies
increase exponentially, worlds spin in place.
Nebulas arise, stretch out across

an infinite sight to hold each one in his mind.
Gently, benevolently, he nurtures them all,
tracing them in perfectly.

Pulls in dark energy from the formless void
of space to form constellations, humankind
may one-day name in celebration.

Nebulas shimmer in and out, casting a radiance
across parsecs, trillions of light years
in distance, measured parallax angles.

Shielded by celestial beings, who move upon
patterns of light, from one far edge of creation
to another with a single thought.

Tender as a whisper caught inside one breath, they
dance between esoteric waves of light
renewing creation,

to peer through it finding a young child lost and
alone, gathering bands of archangels' aid. Watching
over her, as they watch over all of creation.

Unseen by mortal flesh and eyes, imagine it arranged
in open unity. The wizard smiles, one child is
found, another born fresh and new.

Creation arises out of the Nirvana of all likelihoods,
heaven sent. Close your eyes, say
a quiet prayer in blessing.

Keep, each sacred moment of your being.
Here within, where all time merges into
this abiding instant.

We cannot name it or want it to be named,
only see it as a wonderment, dwelling inward
in cycles of the soul, held within our midst.

RUNNING WITH WOLVES

Let us run with the wolves of desire and memory.
Where we are not that far removed from the wildness

that still clings to us in dreams unfolding, before
mirrors white with winter. Across worlds where

ancestors inhabit our bodies with breath and
spirit, who breathe together through

a veiled gate that marks an entrance to eternity.
Nothing is lost here, nothing we do not already

know in the bright bones of our memories.
We remember well, the taste of Eden, which is

wilder still than our imaginations may even
now envision. Let the oldest wisdom lead

us onward with eyes open wide in wonder,
under a midnight of stars, tracing infinite light

streams of the spirit. Let us bow to the wolves'
bright passing across constellations

of thought and consciousness,
unhurried from one dawn to the next.

WALKING ON DARK WATER
The Myth of Er

Hear the sound of thunder, touch the quaking
  earth, journey into oblivion, drink of forgetfulness,
   and move upward to your birth, fare thee well.

Walk upon this dark water, travel upon the hidden shore.
  No crystal sea, but brown and thick as southern
   molasses, lost souls grabbing at your ankles.

It is not an easy thing to be done, water
  cold and icy. Pitching back and forth
   like a ship lost at sea where one

may easily lose their balance. And far
  from what anyone may imagine, there
   is no miracle at work here, only hard work.

Like raising the dead, a hard resurrection,
  many resurrections. Dancing with
   the blind dead that cannot see,

or hear, the dead who
  do not wish to live in any form,
   make it twice as hard.

Would you really, even if you could, come
  back into this life, here, now? I would, yes.
   What I've learned is that you must talk to

each soul alone, walk them away from the
  darkest waters, on to the shore,
   away to firm ground, away from

what the dead have always known.
There's a trick to it all! Calling out
to the dead, loving them, letting life

take root once more. And then erasing
their memories as a kind of mercy the gods
have shown, Lethe, the waters of forgetfulness.

If I had a choice, I'd forget forgetfulness and
drink the waters from Mnemosyne. I'd hold on
to every memory; I'd recall it all and then some.

Lethe [lee-thee]
Mnemosyne [nee-moss-uh-nee]

AFTERWORD

Every poet I know has a story to tell, and tell their stories through the formation of a personal mythology. As we travel through life, our life changes. Our sense of identity shifts with the seasons and people in our life. This is the impermanence of the self; Buddhist philosophy teaches.

Śūnyatā–Nirvana–Emptiness, written of in the Heart Sutra points towards this impermanence, which teaches that our sense of self as being permanent is false. And that the self we may actively identify with is empty of such permanence. Buddhism refers to this as not-self, or no-self, anattā (uhn-uht-tah), it is an ego clinging self, which leads to suffering, misperceptions, and artificial projections.

In the Christian tradition, there is a similar concept, kenosis, the Greek word for emptiness. Kenosis is 'self-emptying' one's own will in becoming receptive to the divine, to be in unity with the divine. Both heaven and nirvana are alike when we understand them as a spiritual path towards union with the divine ultimate mystery out of which all things arise.

In writing a poem, the poet goes through multiple stages and feelings, crafting their words together, until the poem itself comes to an end. A poem is never quite finished. It is almost always incomplete in some sense. The poet simply has to let go of it and trust that the creative process goes on within the people who may read their humble efforts.

All our works as poets and writers are a continuation of other works that came before us, the voices of humanity that have been passed down from one generation to another.

We are simple gatherers who have gathered from those poets, writers, and storytellers, who came before us. Even the greatest among us have been inspired through learning and reading the literary works of humankind. And we, we humble few, are following in their footsteps.

There is something more going on of course. Each poem, in and of itself, begins in silence, in stillness, in an empty space waiting to be filled, on a blank page, or as an even deeper divine memory perhaps. And we, we are full participants in its creation. It is a deeper mystery at work, an inspiration. To be creatively inspired, is to be filled by the spirit of something more, something beyond the mundane.

As much as any poem we write is our own work, it is also not our work. We have been inspired. We have heard the whisperings of God. And at present, at this moment in time, we are merely giving back to humankind the voices who have spoken before in a newer voice.

There are perhaps no accidents in life, just a continuation of one life into and with another, in a continuation of consciousness grounded in the non-duality of God the divine. Where we are grounded in a greater mystery of creation, we cannot quite name, written within us. The Holy Spirit perhaps praying in and with and through us, when we know not how to prayer ourselves.

The words we share are not our own, they have been seen and heard before. They rest in a universal divine consciousness that dwells within. They were written upon our soul's memory, deep within our spirit, in our hearts and minds long ago.

And now, now we have been inspired to return them to humankind, in a healing for humankind. The poet within us has listened deeply to the stillness and silence of creation, and out of this listening, comes a word, a verse, a poem. Each poem written, is an act of creation, a loving act, an act of healing and repairing the world. Tikkun Olam.

"In the beginning was the Word, and the Word was with God, and the Word was God. He was with God in the beginning. Through him all things were made; without him nothing was made that has been made. In him was life, and that life was the light of all mankind. The light shines in the darkness, and the darkness has not overcome it." - John 1 (NRSV)

YOU TOO, ARE THIS LIGHT. ~ RON STARBUCK

ABOUT THE AUTHOR

RON STARBUCK is an EPISCOPALIAN, a Poet and Writer, and the Publisher CEO of Saint Julian Press.

AUTHOR of *There Is Something About Being An Episcopalian*, *When Angels Are Born*, and *Wheels Turning Inward*, three rich collections of poetry, following a poet's mythic and spiritual journey that crosses easily onto the paths of many contemplative traditions. Ron has been deeply engaged in an Interfaith-Buddhist-Christian dialogue for many years, and holds a lifelong interest in literature, poetry, mysticism, comparative religion, theology, and various forms of contemplative practice.

HE has been a contributing writer for *Parabola Magazine*. And has had poems and essays published in *Tiferet: A Journal of Spiritual Literature*, an interview and poem in *The Criterion: An Online International Journal in English*, *The Enchanting Verses Literary Review*, *ONE* from MillerWords Press (Feb. 2016), and *Pirene's Fountain, Volume 7 Issue 15,* from Glass Lyre Press (Oct. 2014). A collection of essays, poems, short stories, audio recordings, and films are available on the Saint Julian Press, Inc., website under Interconnections.

FORMING a new literary press to work with emerging and established writers and poets, and tendering new introductions to the world at large in the framework of an interfaith and cross cultural literary dialogue has been a long-time dream.

To learn more go to SAINTJULIANPRESS.COM.

ACKNOWLEDGMENTS

The selected poems THERE IS SOMETHING ABOUT BEING AN EPISCOPALIAN, GOD'S LONGING, RUMI, ON THE THIRD MORNING, THE JESUS PRAYER FLAG, THEOSIS, A MOCKINGBIRD'S SONG, MOCKINGBIRD MORNING, and ŚŪNYATĀ – EMPTINESS IS FORM; FORM IS EMPTINESS, were first published in *Wheels Turning Inward*, Friesen Press (Aug. 2010).

The poems WIZARD & WHITEFACE CLOWN–ZEN PRIEST and RUNNING WITH WOLVES, first appeared in *PIRENE'S FOUNTAIN, VOLUME 7 ISSUE 15* (Oct. 2014), from Glass Lyre Press.

NOTES

Dedication is from the DUINO ELEGIES, the Tenth Elegy by RAINER MARIA RILKE – Translated by A. S. Kline © 2001

EPIGRAPH – MATTHEW 6:22 – 21st Century King James Version (KJ21) Copyright © 1994 by Deuel Enterprises, Inc.

In the poem, "COMPOSING THE FIRST GRACE," the ending quote is from Paul Tillich's sermon "You Are Accepted," from *THE SHAKING OF THE FOUNDATIONS*, chapter nineteen.

www.ingramcontent.com/pod-product-compliance
Lightning Source LLC
Chambersburg PA
CBHW051842040426
42447CB00006B/650